MEL BAY PRESENTS

# THE GUITARIST'S GUIDE TO FINGERNAILS

## BY RICO STOVER

1 2 3 4 5 6 7 8 9 0

*Visit us on the Web at www.melbay.com — E-mail us at email@melbay.com*

# Table of Contents

# Introduction

The *Guitarist's Guide to Fingernails* provides essential information about your natural nails--how they grow, what factors affect them, how to care for them with products that work as well as analyses of different artificial nail systems currently available, all from a guitarist's point of view.

This book will show you the way to achieve optimum health and strength in your fingernails. It also presents an alternative to artificial nail systems that expose the wearer to toxic substances.

My need for good fingernails has always paralleled my need to play the guitar; they are interconnected. Unfortunately, my fingernails are not naturally good. Frustration with my nail problems compelled me to keep searching for a solution and, after many years of trial and error, I developed a "cure" which I'll share in this book.

*Rico Stover*

# Foreword

Evolution did not give us fingernails for the purpose of playing the guitar, but they sure work great if they are tough enough and of the right length!

This book is dedicated to all guitarists who want to improve their fingernails. To achieve this, you must:

1) Educate yourself about your fingernails and learn how to care for them.
2) Acquire the necessary products.
3) Maintain a system that works.

The key lies in understanding the physiology of your fingernails, what elements affect them adversely and how to deal with them. There are many fine products available today which make it easier than ever to achieve good nails. This book identifies those products and tells you how to obtain them.

A new system for utilizing false nails without toxic glues is also presented here. This system may prove to be revolutionary for guitarists who wish to escape the inevitable "toxic cycle" of current artificial nail systems. Now guitarists can put on a false nail, play x number of hours, then remove the false nail with no harmful side effects. In other words, *it is possible to use artificial nails without ruining your natural nails.*

# Chapter 1: Fingernails
# Finding the Answers

At the bottom of this whole question of nails, one must assess his or her situation and needs, and use what will work. I know that there are many styles of guitar, and many differing ideas on aesthetics of tone. Of course, everyone's fingernails are different. Some guitarists have nails with problematic dips at the end, while some may have a nail that is weaker, and some just have lousy nails due to heredity. Most people, however, have poor nail quality due to lack of proper care.

You can care for your nails in a meaningful way only if you understand what affects them and how to address specific issues. To begin with, there are two major concepts to comprehend:

**I. Everything that touches your nails affects them.**

**II. Lack of Moisture** and **Loosening of Keratin Protein Fibers** are your nails' main enemies.

**Did you know that simply running tap water over your nails affects them?**

Your fingernails are in a "war zone". Every day they are incessantly subjected to all kinds of assaults in the form of liquids, chemicals and physical shock. Exposure to anything chemical in any form will affect your fingernails. And everything we touch is in fact a chemical (save light and electricity). There are many potentially harmful or debilitating substances and liquids out there just waiting to touch or permeate our nail, including chlorine, cleaning products, detergents, soaps and certain cosmetics to name a few of the primary offenders.

Maybe, thanks to "natural heredity", you are one of those lucky people who have nails that are thick, strong and resilient—the kind that hold up well no matter what. Congratulations! My nails are not thick and I have always had a variety of problems with them; they would get too thin when I played a lot (particularly *rasgueado* playing) and they also tended to wear away at the outer edge at the spot where contact was made with the string.

Consequently, I had to resort to using artificial nails. This of course always carried with it an inevitable negative effect on my real fingernail. I began to wish that I could either grow better nails or else find out how to attach false nails without using a toxic substance for the adhesive. I kept searching and in the end I found the answers to both problems.

The good news is that you really can do something about problem fingernails that will make a big difference. That is guaranteed. In view of the large selection of nail care products available today, there is no excuse why anyone should have poor nails. There are hundreds of products available and some of the better ones are discussed in Chapter Three. For now, we need to take a look at what makes a healthy fingernail.

## Understanding Your Fingernails

Fingernails are made of *keratin*, as are the hair and skin (which are much softer and more flexible forms of it). Keratin is defined as "a highly insoluble albuminous compound containing sulfur that forms the essential ingredient of horns, claws, nails, etc." "Albuminous" refers to certain proteins found in the blood which are soluble in water and are coagulated by heat, alcohol and the stronger acids. Keratin is the same stuff that forms the feathers and beaks of birds, the shells of turtles, lobsters and crabs, and the scales of fish and reptiles.

o your nails are actually protein. Nails are in fact a part of the *epidermis* or outer layer of skin. Our nails grow n top of a *nail bed*. Healthy nail beds are pink which indicate not only a rich blood supply to the area, but our eneral good health as well. The nails are the last areas of the body to receive oxygen and nutrients carried in e blood, and will often show signs of deficiencies sooner than tissues receiving sufficient nutrients. Fingernails n reveal a good deal about the body's internal health; that's why physicians often look at our nails as part of general physical exam. At least 40 potential medical problems can be detected when your doctor examines ur fingernails.

bnormalities or changes in the nails and nail beds can sometimes be the result of nutritional deficiencies, or ay indicate some underlying condition. Risk factors for the development of nail abnormalities include exces-ve exposure to water and solvents, trauma to the nails, irritants, drug exposure, infections, dermatologic con-itions and disease of the pulmonary, cardiovascular or gastrointestinal systems. If your nail problems are caused y something more serious than "dryness and keratin thinning", then obviously you should see a doctor and seek medical solution to the specific problem.

# ingernail Anatomy

he nail is divided into six specific parts: the root, nail bed, nail plate, eponychium (cuticle), perionychium, and yponychium.

## ail Root

he root of the fingernail is also known as the *germinal matrix*. This portion of the nail is actually beneath the kin behind the fingernail and extends several millimeters into the finger. The fingernail root produces most of e volume of the nail and the nail bed. The edge of the germinal matrix is seen as a white, crescent shaped struc-ire called the *lunula*.

## ail Bed

he nail bed is also called the *sterile matrix*. It extends from the edge of the lunula to the fingertip. The nail bed ontains blood vessels, nerves, and melanocytes (melanin producing cells). As the nail is generated by the root, streams down along the nail bed, which adds material to the undersurface of the nail making it thicker.

## ail Plate

he nail plate is what we commonly call the "fingernail". It grows as if in a three-sided tunnel with no roof and held together by strong, interconnecting bands of keratin. The nail plate consists of three layers:

**Dorsal Layer:** The topmost layer of the plate. Its cells are primarily soft keratin and are less flat than nail cells of the intermediate layer below it.

**Intermediate Layer:** The middle layer of the nail plate. Its cells are primarily hard keratin and are flatter, larger, and more compact than nail cells above or below it. The keratin fibers here are arranged parallel to the lunula at the base of each nail.

**Ventral Layer:** The bottom layer of the nail plate. Its cells are primarily made of soft keratin and its thick-ness is similar to the dorsal layer.

he nail cells forming these three layers of the nail plate are bound to each other by numerous tiny protein fibers. he randomly arranged keratin fibers in the two outer layers give each nail its bending strength (*Journal of Experimental Biology*, vol. 207, p. 735). It is the diminishing of these fibers that makes our nails thin.

*Alpha-keratin* has long molecules made up of chains of thousands of atoms. Each link in the molecular chain is comprised of a pair of carbon atoms and a nitrogen atom which join the links together. The bonds between these atoms are pairs of electrons. Other atoms, called *sidechains*, are bonded to the atoms of the main chain like charms on a bracelet. Keratin molecules are twisted together in threes like strands of a rope. The strands are held together by bridges made from sulfur atom side-chains. The sulfur atoms on one protein strand are bonded to the sulfur atoms on the neighboring strand by a pair of electrons and this three dimensional network toughens the fingernail.

Proteins can be thought of as long chains that can be tied together like the rungs on a ladder to form a "cross-linkage". When keratin is heated or shocked the sulfur bonds break leaving a single, "unpaired" electron on each sulfur atom. The end result is diminished thickness of keratin in the nail plate.

The nail plate is kept flexible by a sticky residue of oils and moisture that constantly flows upward from the nail bed. This residue creates a matte shine on the surface of the plate and is a major factor in nail plate flexibility. This natural "residue of oils", which diminishes as you age, is always being minimized by exposure of the nails to water, detergents, solvents, etc.

The linkage between the keratin levels gives the nail plate strength, while the oils and moisture form the "cement" that holds the nail plate cells together and keep them well lubricated, resulting in a strong flexible nail.

### Eponychium (Cuticle)
The *eponychium* is situated between the skin of the finger and the nail plate fusing these structures together. It is not advisable to "trim the cuticle" because it does function as a barrier against water and bacteria.

### Perionychium
The *perioncyhium* is the skin that overlies the nail plate on its sides. It is also known as the paronychial edge. The perionychium is the site of hangnails, ingrown nails, and an infection of the skin called *paronychia* that can be painful.

### Hyponychium
The *hyponychium* is the area between the nail plate and the fingertip. It is the junction between the free edge of the nail and the skin of the fingertip, also providing a waterproof barrier.

### Free Border or Free Edge
The part of the nail that extends outward from the fingertip (the part you have to file or sand).

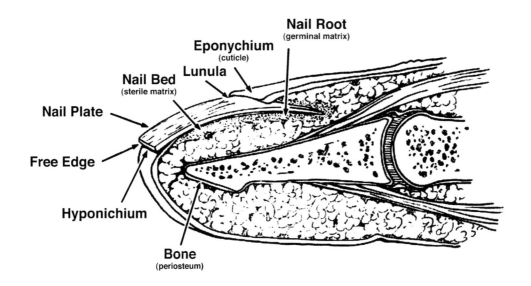

# Healthy Nail Characteristics

Healthy nails possess a combination of strength, hardness and flexibility. **Strength** shows how likely the plate is to break under force. **Hardness** measures how easily the plate is dented or scratched. **Flexibility** determines how much the plate will bend. **Toughness** is a combination of these three properties. The combination of strength and flexibility create the ideal nail plate. Many factors can cause changes in the nail plate, resulting in lowered levels of strength and flexibility. For instance, water may be absorbed by the nail plate causing the cells to shift and change shape.

After nail cells are formed at the germinal matrix they progressively become harder, broaden and flatten as they move toward the fingertip. The oldest cells are the most compact, making the nail plate harder and more dense closest to the free edge. The plate rides forward on the nail bed in a "rail and groove" effect, much like a train riding on its tracks. As we grow older, the nail bed produces less oil and moisture, and this rail and groove effect becomes evident as vertical ridges in the plate.

# More Nail Facts

As children, our fingernails and toenails grow an average of two inches per year. But as we age, our nails grow more slowly. As adults, our fingernails grow only about an <u>inch in eight months</u>. Nails grow approximately one-half to <u>one millimeter</u> weekly (about 0.1 mm per day). While growth rates can vary with age, season and nutrition, it takes from <u>five</u> to <u>seven months</u> for the nail plate to completely replace itself.

William B. Bean studied his own nail growth for 35 years and published the data in *Arch Intern Med*, 1974, Vol. 134, 497-502 (30 years of growth) and ibid, 1980, Vol. 140, p. 73-76 (35 years of growth). He found that his nails grow more slowly with age; his nail growth rate at age 32 was 0.123mm/day, but by age 67 had decreased to 0.095mm/day. Neither geographical location nor physical activity appeared to have any significant effects.

Nails reputedly grow faster during the summer. The <u>middle fingernail grows</u> fastest, with the growth rate progressively decreasing on the ring, index, and little fingers and finally the <u>thumb</u>. Right-handed people's nails grow more quickly on the right hand and vice versa.

When a nail is injured and falls off, it is replaced at the normal growth rate. However, if the germinal matrix is destroyed, the new nail will not grow. If the matrix is damaged, the new nail is likely to grow in a distorted form.

# Two Villains

As stated above, most nail problems--dryness, cracking, flaking, eroding or splitting—are due mainly to two "villains" that are always on the scene that must be dealt with every day:

1. **loss of moisture** in the nail (the inevitable effect of aging and exposure to chemicals)
2. **loosening of the keratin protein fibers** in the nail plate (from exposure to chemicals)

Keratin is tough and resists most environmental stresses, but like hair is damaged by alkaline conditions, excessive heat and exposure to solvents. If you could wear a glove all the time on your playing hand and also never have to wash that hand, your nails would stand a chance against our two "villains". But obviously this is not a realistic solution. So what can you do?

The answer is to apply pure **OILS** from plant sources. Below is a list of the most common and accessible pure oils, all of which are beneficial to apply directly to your nails. **Mineral oil** is less effective as its ability to be absorbed is limited due to the large size of its molecules. **Vitamin E** <u>is very good, so is</u> **liquid lanolin**. Sometimes I take a **clove of garlic** and stick my nail deep into it and leave it there for a bit. This is good for the nail because garlic has abundant oils and kills bacteria. You get the idea; the more oils and the more often you use them, the better for the health of your nails.

*Every time you get your hands wet, oil your nails immediately after drying your hands.*

Unless you understand the fact that **dryness** is your constant enemy, your nails will show little improvement.

# Diet

I have noticed that orally ingesting **caplets of flax seed oil** and **MSM** (methylsulfonylmethane) really helps. MSM is available in special supplemental blends that include such nail friendly ingredients as silica, gotu kola, carrot powder and so on.

**Biotin**, which is part of the vitamin B complex, is also very beneficial to take. In a study in Germany, 60 patients who had poor nail quality, but had no overt biotin deficiency, were treated for 6 months with 2.5 mg of biotin per day and the improvement in nail quality was significant compared to the placebo group. ("The Influence of Biotin on Nails of Reduced Quality" *Aktuelle Dermatologie* (Germany), 1996, 22/1-2 (20-24). Note that this study used a relatively large dosage of biotin at 2.5 milligrams every day.

Some people erroneously believe that eating certain foods or using special creams or lotions will increase nail growth rate. Although the nail plate requires certain nutrients for proper growth, there is very little evidence that eating any particular food will cause it to grow faster. Numerous creams, oils and lotions are sold as "growth accelerators", a claim which some dispute as false and misleading, pointing out that only stringently tested medicinal drugs can make such claims.

The growth accelerator issue is to some degree an open question. True, those products that bill themselves as growth accelerators and that use principally chemicals in their formulation are in fact not very effective. Indeed, by using such products you would be putting on your nails certain substances that you would be better off without. There is one company, however, which offers "proof" that their product does in fact accelerate nail growth: the "CP Nail Renewal System" from the Skin Biology Corporation, which makes beauty products with copper peptides as a principal ingredient. They took two groups of people and treated one hand with the CP System and the other with a placebo. In both groups the nails on the treated hand were longer (see www.skinbio.com for a summary of test results).

**Calcium** can also be beneficial. It is an important component of your nails, hair and bones, and when you buy a supplement look for "elemental calcium" on the label, which indicates how much of the calcium in the product your body will absorb. If you see "USP" on the label it means that the standards for absorption have been met. You may also wish to adjust your diet to augment your mineral intake with such high calcium-magnesium-iron foods as dark leafy greens.

Taking **gelatin** may or may not be effective, depending upon whom you consult. I took gelatin and did not notice any significant difference. Some say it makes a difference. Keep in mind that it may take six to eight weeks to notice the effect of dietary changes.

# General Nutrition

. Eat a well balanced diet, low in fat, with plenty of fruits and vegetables and foods that are rich in iron, calcium, vitamin B and potassium, like dairy products, seafood, celery, and soy.

. Drink 8 glasses of water every day to hydrate the body, including your nails. Weak and splitting nails can sometimes be traced to poor water intake.

**Vitamins and Minerals** - especially vitamins A and C, calcium, magnesium, zinc, manganese, iron
**Herbs and Phytonutrients** - horsetail, lecithin, gelatin, bioflavonoids
**Antioxidants** - especially vitamin E
**Essential Fatty Acids** - omega-3 and omega-6 (from flax seed oil)

My program for achieving healthy nails boils down to this:

) Use oils and other products to lubricate the nails every day.
) Stop using toxic substances.
) Improve your diet.

## Some Everyday Tips:

Try using your left hand (if you are a right-handed player and vice versa) for certain things involving water, like when you rinse out a bowl in the sink or brush your teeth. The less water on your nails, the better.

f you are going to do any cleaning or yard work, wear a glove on your playing hand.

f you work with solvents like gasoline or kerosine, etc., definitely wear gloves.

f you handle paper for prolonged periods of time on a daily basis, this can be a significant factor in zapping moisture from your nails.

f you spend a lot of time in a swimming pool, good luck. You must really be vigilant to counteract the debilitating effects of constant immersion of your nails in highly chlorinated water.

# Chapter 2: Artificial Fingernails

It's no secret that false nails can work well for playing the guitar. As I see it, there are three basic reasons why a guitarist would use artificial nails:

1) Your natural nails are not good.
2) You've had an accident and cracked or damaged a real nail.
3) You like the sound of artificial nails better.

## Artificial Nail Systems

There are five types of artificial fingernails:

**Acrylic systems** use powdered polymer and liquid monomer which are mixed together. The powder and liquid react to form a plastic paste. This paste is smoothed onto the nail, where it cures, or hardens, at room temperature. Sometimes benzoyl peroxide is included to make the plastic harden faster.

**Porcelain Nails** are like acrylic nails, except that they use a finely ground, glass-like material in the powder.

### Gel Systems

In gel systems, layers of resin are applied to the nail; these layers combine to form a solid nail. There are several different kinds of gels; all of them harden when exposed to light. The original formulas were hardened with ultraviolet light; newer formulas harden under ordinary room lighting (called white light). Some gel systems use layers of different resins, while others use layers of a single resin.

### Wraps

Fiberglass, linen and silk wraps are all based upon the same process. A fabric mesh is fixed in place with an adhesive; then a sealant is applied to help keep out moisture and discourage lifting. The new nail is then sanded and filed to the desired shape and length.

### Tips

Plastic nail shapes called tips are glued over the natural nail. These "preformed nails" sometimes cover the nail from the cuticle to the free edge, but more frequently they are applied midway down the nail plate. A cyano-acrylate glue is used to adhere the plastic shape to the nail. Acrylics, gels, or wraps may then be applied to smooth and strengthen the final form.

## Artificial Nail Systems for Guitarists

### guitarplayernails.com

This is kind of an update to the "ping pong ball" method, which many guitarists still use. Instead of ping pong ball material, this company sends you a durable plastic material (called "Instant Nail") that you cut in the shape of the nail, glue on to your real nail with cyanoacrilate, and then shape accordingly with a file and sandpaper. The nail material provided is in the form of a flat sheet. As the real nail is covered and cyanoacrilate is applied, guitarplayernails.com is classified as a "toxic/cover" solution.

### Miro Nail System

Miro Simic of Sweden is a guitarist who has developed a wrap nail care system that consists of a self-adhesive silk wrap which you cut and form, and then glue to your nails with a "resin" glue consisting of hydroquinone and ethyl

...yanoacrilate. The kit includes a bottle with 17 different natural and essential oils which you apply to your nails ...vice a day. You also get a 4-step buffer (polisher) for forming and polishing your nails. These wrap nails will stand ...p to water and hold, even if you take a bath or do the dishes, etc. It is commendable that Simic provides a blend of ...ls to apply to the nail, but, this is essentially another "toxic/cover" solution.

## ...ower Nails

...his is a gel system sold only by Carlos Juan (www.american-guitar-center.com) who provides everything you ...eed to apply and maintain nails covered with gel. It is a deluxe kit that costs over three hundred dollars. ...ncluded in the Power Nails kit are an ultrabond applicator, a pen applicator, 15 grams of thick viscosity UV gel, ...leaner, brush cleaner, timer clock, model supports, double sided files, modeling brushes, wooden manicure ...tick, and a 155 or 230-volt mirror lined UV-lamp. This is an elaborate "do it yourself" system of high quality... ...ut in the final analysis, it is yet another "toxic/cover" solution.

## ...avarez Nail Kit

...his is a silk wrap system that uses cyanoacrilate. It works quite well to repair a damaged nail.

## ...ing Pong Ball

...he longstanding homemade method of putting on a fake nail: cut a ping pong ball to the desired shape, glue it ...n, sand and buff, and reinforce with several layers of super glue, and there you have it!

# ...he Toxic/Cover Dilemma

...ll of the artificial nail systems described above have three things in common:
1) They **cover** the surface of the real nail either totally or partially.
2) They all require the use of **toxic substances**.
3) The real nail stays **permanently covered**.

...have tried silk wraps, as well as numerous kinds of preformed tips. I also used acrylic nails, porcelain nails and ...els for several years before I abandoned them. My feelings were that they were relatively expensive to main-...ain, problematic as regards thickness and shape, and of course, the health of my real nails suffered terribly...in ...he end they were very thin and soft.

...My nail health was compromised because acrylics have the characteristic of coming loose in their bond with the ...eal nail surface after a couple of weeks, particularly at the edges. This necessitates stripping away that part of ...he acrylic that has come loose and filling it in with fresh acrylic. When the hardened acrylic separates from the ...eal nail, it takes with it a small amount of that top layer of keratin that forms the dorsal layer. Repeating this ...over and over for an extended period causes the nail to become progressively thinner with diminished hardness. ...ven if you stopped using the acrylics, it would take several months for your real nails to grow out and playing ...without nails, no matter what the reason, is certainly intolerable if you play frequently. So you embrace the **toxic ...ycle**. Once you are in it, escaping it is very difficult. **The toxic cycle is self perpetuating**.

...ll of these toxic chemicals—acetone, cyanoacrilate ester glue, epoxy, nail polish, acrylics, cleaning solvents, ...ast drying agents, etc.—all are very bad for the human body. And to breathe them for a prolonged period of ...ime, like those poor ladies that work in the beauty salons doing acrylic nails all day—this is playing Russian ...oulette with your health! No thank you. Something in my intuition tells me that **all toxic substances should be ...voided** (except rubbing alcohol which works ok for cleaning your nails when necessary).

...Your fingernails, like your skin, are porous and allow things to enter into the body through them. Thus, contin-...ually bathing or covering your nail surfaces with these chemicals not only debilitates the natural nail, but puts one at risk for possible negative side effects from the exposure to these chemicals. Exposure to acetone, for example, can cause nerve damage, contribute to diabetes and other metabolic disorders, and can create such symptoms in the body as: blood poisoning, dizziness, drowsiness, gastritis, headaches, increased heart rate, impaired reflexes, incoordination, inflammation of stomach, liver injury, loss of sensation, nausea, pneumonia, respiratory failure, restlessness, shock, slurred speech, stupor, vomiting and weakness. Over-exposure to acetone has also been related to low birth rate, cataracts, coma and death. Need I say more?

Real nails do not fare well at all when they are covered with anything—be it acrylics, cyanoacrilate glue, nail polish, silk wraps, etc. When habitually covered, the real nail tends to get softer and doesn't have as much "structural integrity" as a normal healthy nail. Once you start putting these toxic materials on your real nail surfaces, their general state of healthiness will in fact decline. Your real nail will never be "normal" if you keep it constantly covered up. It's that simple. Your nails were not meant to be covered over with anything really—they are what is left of the mammalian claw and you know what they were used for!

A professional guitarist friend of mine has developed a "limited" toxic/cover technique: he puts cyanoacrilate only on the very ends of his fingernails at the free edge, then he dips those edges into acrylic powder. This dries and hardens, forming a tough ridge over the free edge area, which he then sands and polishes. The net effect is that his nails are strong at the edge but stay relatively healthy because they are not covered with anything toxic as they grow outward from the matrix.

**The ultimate artificial nail:** located in Utah, **True Fit Nails** offers what may be the most sophisticated artificial nails system. In this system, your natural nails are scanned into their computer, then they make the false nails on premises using the exact dimensions of your real nails. They are very tough and will last a long time. This procedure is expensive up front but actually, compared to what you might spend on having acrylics done for a year or two, it is not all that unreasonable.

## Artificial Nails: Some Afterthoughts

In 1938 the United States government passed the Food, Drug and Cosmetic Act, which defined "cosmetics" as products for cleaning, beautifying, promoting attractiveness or altering appearance. They were not defined by their ingredients, but rather by their function. See "Cosmetic Safety: More Complex Than at First Blush" in the November 1991 *FDA Consumer*.

Unlike drugs, cosmetics are largely unregulated. They are not required to be tested by the Food and Drug Administration or by any other governmental agency before they are released on the market. Another way of looking at it: we as consumers are test "guinea pigs" for cosmetic products.

To illustrate this, here is a list of the chemicals that you are exposed to when you have acrylic nails applied: acetone, benzene, benzoyl peroxide powder, butyl methacrylate liquid, ethyl acetate, ethyl cyanoacrylate, ethyl methacrylate liquid, hydroquinone primer, isobutyl methacrylate liquid, 4-methoxyphenol, methyl ethyl ketone primer, neoprene, titanium dioxide and toluene--fourteen different chemicals!

Acrylic nails were introduced about 30 years ago and have grown in popularity tremendously in the last few years. The net effects of people being exposed to all the chemicals involved with the application and maintenance of any of these toxic/cover systems are in truth an unknown at this time, but it is not unreasonable to suspect that there are potentially serious **health risks** involved with all these systems and that ongoing research will eventually corroborate this fact.

Only in rare situations has the FDA stepped in and banned a cosmetic product, as with *methyl methacrilate* (MMA), one of the three kinds of acrilates used in acrylic nails. In 1974 the FDA declared it to be a "**poisonous** nd deleterious substance when used on fingernails". Responsible manufacturers quickly and voluntarily switched their salon clients over to ethyl methacrylate (EMA), a more expensive and "safer" bonding liquid. Reputable nail salons followed suit. The difference between EMA and MMA is the same as the difference between wood alcohol (methanol) and beverage alcohol (ethanol). Wood alcohol can kill you while beverage alcohol is considered safe if not used in excess!

Banning a product is one thing. Enforcing that ban is quite another. It is claimed that there are still many nail salons that use MMA and lie about it because MMA is quite a bit less expensive than EMA. And since there is no real enforcement at the thousands of nail salons across the US and the world, you just may be at risk....

Another serious problem associated with using false nails is a **buildup of bacteria** and/or **growth of fungus** (onychomycosis). Clinical studies have demonstrated that this is a very real potential side effect of long term usage of false nails. This bacteria has caused repercussions in the health care industry (hospitals) and in the food service industry, such that workers in these professions are now prohibited from wearing artificial nails. It is yet another negative potential associated with "toxic/cover" methods.

In truth, the entire artificial nail industry is suspect because the user is exposed to toxic and even lethal chemicals in some form or other that in fact do not aid in or improve the health of the natural nail. For that reason alone, I am against using acrylic, porcelain, gel and wrap systems. I am not against using preformed false nails per se if they can be attached without a toxic glue (which is now possible).

When you see a nail care product and pick up the box or bottle and scrutinize the contents, if the first few ingredients are "chemical" names like butyl acetate, ethyl acetate, polyquarternium-11, toluene, etc., put it back on the shelf. Such products are bad for the nails, no matter what the label says. It is a sobering fact that certain organic chemicals and solvents can permeate the skin and nails and enter directly into the bloodstream with the potential to reach the liver, kidneys, brain and other tissues.

As regards any commercial nail product, ask yourself:

*Can I also put this on my skin with no problems?*

If you cannot, then leave it alone.

In spite of all these drawbacks, if you are happy with acrylics or whatever you are using, and you don't particularly care about your real nail or any of the potential health hazards...then there is no problem. If it works, OK. That's great. I can appreciate that fact. You need not read further.

But if you want to play the guitar with your real nails and escape the trap of synthetic toxic systems, then read on.

# Chapter 3: Natural Nail Care Products

If you use any of the products featured in this chapter, your nails will improve. I classify these products into three categories:

A.  moisturizers
B.  nail fortifiers/hardeners
C.  nail growth stimulators

## Moisturizing Products

Products that are effective for keeping your nails well lubricated fall into three basic categories:

**Pure Oils**
**Oil-Based Products**
**Special Source Moisturizers**

### 1. Pure Oils

Here are some of the better pure oils that can be beneficial with regular use: **almond, apricot, avocado, borage seed, calendula, camellia, grapeseed, jojoba, neem leaf, olive, peach, peanut, sesame, walnut** and **wheat germ**. **Emu oil** is an animal source oil that is touted as beneficial for the nails and skin. You can obtain most of these pure oils without too much difficulty either in your local health food store/supermarket or on the Internet.

Do not confuse "**pure oils**" with "**essential oils**". They are not the same by any means. *Essential oils* are the subtle, volatile liquids that are produced in various glands and sacs within aromatic plants, shrubs, flowers, trees, bushes and seeds. Depending on the plant species, oils are extracted from the petals, leaves, roots, buds, twigs, rhizomes, wood, bark, resin or fruit of the plant. In most cases essential oils are 75 to 100 times more concentrated than the oils found in dried herbs. These "oils", which in the majority of cases are clear and volatile type liquids, contain hundreds of organic constituents that combine together to work on many different levels and are the central part of **aromatherapy** treatment.

Essential oils should never be applied directly to the nails (or any part of the body). They are so powerful that they must always be mixed in a ratio of 2% essential oil to 98% pure oil (called a "carrier oil" in aromatherapy). A good example would be the essential oil made from the **myrrh plant**, which is very good for fingernails, but which must be combined with, for example, jojoba, peanut or almond oil for use.

### 2. Oil Based Products

Below are listed products that blend oils with other ingredients. All of these products differ in their makeup, but they all have oils as primary ingredients. They "smell nice" too, which is another reason why these oil blend products exist, as some natural oils have a fragrance that may be "commercially unappealing" by their nature.

#### Badger Lip and Body Balm
This salve is also an excellent moisturizer for the nails as it contains olive oil, castor oil, beeswax, extracts of aloe vera, rose hip and sea buckthorn berry, plus essential oils. .75 oz. tin **W. S. Badger Co.**

#### Black Pearl Nail and Cuticle Oil
This product contains neem seed oil, emu oil, hemp seed oil, vitamin E plus essential oils of myrrh, patchouli, cedarwood, lemon eucalyptus, geranium and palmorosa. 1 fl. oz. **Black Pearl Botanicals**.

### Healthy Hoof Cream
The original equestrian formula used by horse trainers contains deionized water, glycerin, stearic acid, soybean oil, lanolin, hydrogenated cotton seed glyceride, bees wax, polysorbate 20, aloe vera, cetyl alcohol, triethanolamine, rosemary oil, dimethicone, lavender oil, methylparaben, propylparaben, hydrolyzed protein, allantoin, castor oil, tetrasodium EDTA, FD#C Yellow #5, FD&C Yellow #6. 4 fl. oz. **Gena Laboratories.**

### Isabella Nail Oil
This product is a wonderful blend of peanut oil, jojoba oil, neem oil, vitamin E oil, fragrance (essential oils), lavender oil and chamomile oil. **Isabella.**

### Nail Advantage Restore
A unique blend of whole leaf aloe vera, apricot kernel oil, tea tree oil, horsetail extract. 1 fl. oz. **HMS Crown, Inc.**

### Nailtiques Oil Therapy
This product is a mixture of 11 oils and I have found it to be a great help at a very reasonable price. Contents: safflower oil, sunflower seed oil, sweet almond oil, peach kernel oil, apricot kernel oil, grape seed oil, walnut oil, avocado oil, sesame oil, wheat germ oil, aloe vera oil, tocopherol (vitamin E), ergocalciferol (vitamin D), ascorbic acid (vitamin C), fragrance, D&C Red No. 17. .25 fl. oz. **Nailtiques Company.**

### Nail Nutrient
A very fine product –highly recommended. Contains avocado oil, grapeseed oil plus essential oils of carrot, lemon and rosemary. .5 fl. oz **Botanical Skin Works.**

### Natural Nail Grow
A mixture of grapeseed oil, jojoba oil, heliocarrot, flaxseed, vitamin E plus pure essential oils of lemon, lavender, peppermint, grapefruit, rosemary and tea tree. 1 fl. oz. **Herbal Luxuries, Inc.**

### Onymyrrhe
The very best product for your nails, number one on my list. Onymyrrhe is the old English name for myrrh and is made entirely from the resin of myrrh plant. The resin is a more concentrated form of myrrh, but it is not an essential oil. (www.onymyrrhe.com) .5 fl. oz **The Tetra Corporation.**

### Proclaim Natural 7 Oil
A nice blend of seven different oils: peanut, castor, canola, fruit oil, wheat germ, sesame, and sweet almond. 8 fl. oz. Very economical. Available only from **Sally's Beauty Supply**.

### Rainbow Research Golden Oil
A very cost effective product consisting of peanut oil, almond oil, olive oil, lanolin and vitamin E. 8 fl. oz. **Rainbow Research Corporation.**

### Smart Nails Lubricating Oil Pen
A blend of ten oils in a portable handy pen form. Contains soybean oil, almond oil, wheat germ oil, tea tree oil, sesame oil, vitamin E, safflower oil, retinol, evening promise oil and ergocalciferol. **Aquarian Treasures.**

*Trementina Healing Balm*
A combination of sap from the piñon tree (called trementina) blended with olive oil and beeswax. This product can also be effective on the calluses of your left hand fingers to prevent them from drying out or cracking. **Wildlands Beauty Products.**

*Venetian Beauty Oil*
A real bargain as oils go, this product contains olive oil, sunflower oil, wheat germ oil, sesame oil and vitamin E but there are 4 varieties of this product available with additional additive oils. The best one for nails is "Olivia's Grace", which adds a blend of sandalwood, rose geranium and myrrh oils. 4.5 oz. **Pisani Company**.

## 3. Special Source Moisturizers
*Source Océan Nourishing Nail and Cuticle Serum*
Contains water, glycerin, solubillisant LRI, hydrogenated castor oil, hydrolyzed keratin, algae extract, hydroxyethyl cellulose, marine hydrolyzed collagen, marine plasma, sodium chondroitin sulfate, marine oligoproteins, marine elastin, panthenol, ascorbyl methyl silanol pectinate, vitamin E, diazolidinyl urea, tetrasodium EDTA, methylchloroisothazolinone and methylisothizolinone, citric acid, fragrance, FD&C blue #1, FD&C yellow #5.

> *Bag Balm*
This product is made up of 8-hydroxyquionoline sulfate in a petrolatum lanolin base. It is sold to dairy farmers to put on the udders of cows! However, it works great on your nails and skin and is absolutely the best bargain when it comes to lanolin-based moisturizers as it comes in a 10 ounce tin that is wide enough for you to dip your nails into it and immerse them. It also works great for the left hand calloused fingertips. **Dairy Association Incorporated.**

*Elon*
A very fine cream that combines lanolin, beeswax, petrolatum, sodium borate and oxyquinoline. It is a great moisturizer for the nails that is not expensive and extremely effective. .25 oz jar **Dartmouth Pharmaceuticals.**

*Natural Nails Growth Formula*
A very effective product that has a lovely fragrance. Contains lanolin, oxyquinoline, beeswax, aeromatics, petrolatum, sodium borate, wintergreen and mustard oil. 1 oz. **Fingernailcare.com.**

*Liquid lanolin* is also very good to rub into your nails. Lanolin has been called "wool grease" and of course comes from sheep. It is extremely effective as a moisturizer on your nails, hair and skin. It is also used in numerous products as the major ingredient, as in the cream Elon cited above.

*Vitamin E* can be obtained in numerous forms. Also called tocopherol, it is very beneficial to the skin and nails whether taken as caplets or applied topically.

I stagger the use of oils and lotions and every day I apply at least 3 different products to my nails. I repeat—**you cannot put too much oil on your nails or skin**. If your routine has you out and about all day, you can try the oil pens recommended in the products list as a small portable solution that can fit in your pocket.

## Nail Fortifier/Hardeners

### Delore Organic Natural Nail Hardener
This product features an unusual blend of soybean oil, wheat germ oil, corn oil, peanut oil, linoleic acid, oleic acid, vitamin E, retinol and ergocalciferol. Beyond its claims as a nail hardener, I find it effective also as a moisturizer. .25 fl. oz. **American International Industries.**

### Hard as Hoof Nail Strengthener Cream
This is a good product that can easily be purchased in the USA in many major chain stores. It works, no doubt because of its natural ingredients: purified water, aloe vera concentrate, jojoba oil, aloe vera oil, glycerin, glyceryl stearate, bees- wax, hydolized protein, calcium panothenate, allantoin, liposomes, vitamins A, C, D & E, di-panthenol, natural fragrance, methyl paraben, propyl paraben. 1 oz. **Onyx Laboratories, Ltd.**

### Nature's Plus Ultra Nail Strengthener
A fine product containing tinctures of calendula, lavender, tea tree and cucumber in an alcohol base plus PVM/MA copolymer, purified water, aloe vera gel, whole wheat protein, vitamin B-1, B-2, niacin, pantothenic acid, vitaimin B-6, B-12, and mucopolysaccharides (from aloe vera). .25 fl. oz. **Nature's Plus.**

### ProStrong ProAccelerator Fluoride Nail Strengthener
Denatured alcohol and ammonium hexalfluorophosphate. The only nail care product with fluoride. .5 fl. oz. **ProStrong, Inc.**

### ProStrong ProCal Calcium Nail Supplement
Denatured alcohol, calcium chloride, glycerin, ethoxydiglycol, Blue 1 (CI 42090), Yellow 5 (CI 19140). .25 fl oz. **ProStrong, Inc.**

### Reconstrux
Ingredients: sunflower seed oil, sesame seed oil, cyclomethicone, borage seed oil, vitamin E, phythantriol, BHT, fragrance. 1/8 fl. oz. **ibd (American International Industries).**

### Trind Nail Balsam
This brush-on liquid is the only product for nails with biotin in it and, though it contains no oils, it is nonetheless very effective. It contains water, denautured alcohol, C12-15 alkyl octanoate, propylene glycol, panthenol, phytantriol, triethanolamine, tocopheryl, acetate, mehtylparaben, caffeine, benzophenone-4, diazolidnyl, urea, carbomer, propylparaben, phospholipids, biotin, laureth-4, allantoin, disodium EDTA, fragrance, Blue 1. .30 fl. oz. **Trind Nail & Hand Corporation.**

## 5. Nail Growth Accelerators

### CP Nail Renewal
A unique blend of copper peptides, retinol, tocotrienols, squalane and octyl palmitate. .5 oz. **Skin Biology Incorporated.**

### Robert McDowell's Fingernail - Growth Stimulating Oil
Contains oils of arnica, bladderack, comfrey, linseed, equisetum, rosemary, and wintergreen. This product claims to improve circulation to the "roots of the nail". 100 ml **Robert McDowell Herbal Treatments.**

# Chapter 4: False Nails
# With a Nontoxic Adhesive

The false nails I use sound really good. In fact, they may sound as good as a real nail, and certainly in downward strumming of *rasgueados* they are more effective than real nails. So I like preformed artificial nails. I do not reject them.

***I do reject using all forms of toxic substances for their adhesion.***

So the question is: how to make them stick without a toxic glue?

I have found an adhesive that does the job. I also have found the best preformed artificial nails to use for guitar playing. The *RICONAIL* system utilizes an adhesive that is nontoxic, nonpermanent and quite effective. The artificial nails provided by *RICONAILS* are of the highest quality and will last for a significantly long time.

*RICONAILS* are available in the ***Emergency Nail Kit***, which contains:
1) 5 preformed false nails in different sizes
2) a synthetic rubber based nontoxic adhesive
3) 1 roll Transpore clear surgical tape

The following instructions must be followed exactly for the *RICONAIL* system to work.

## Using the RICONAIL System

### Step 1: Shaping the Artificial Nails
Each artificial nail must be shortened, trimmed, shaped and polished to the desired length and size as your needs require. This can be done the same way that one does it with a natural nail with files and sandpaper.

The shape and size of the artificial nail should be such that it covers the entire surface of the natural nail, being just a wee bit longer than the free edge of the real nail so as to overlap it. If your nail is short (or even absent) then the adhesive will still work on a diminished nail plate surface.

The back edge of the false nail should fit snugly up against the cuticle with no gap. This is important because a gap can be problematic when doing a downward *rasgueado* as the edge can catch on the string. So the total size of the artificial nail must be such that the back edge fits flush up against the cuticle.

Depending upon the exact shape and curve of your real nails, it may be necessary to make a slight adjustment to a false nail. This has to do with the horizontal curve of the false nail in relation to the curve of your true nail. You want the false nail to fit as flush and as tight as possible against the real nail, and if the arch of the preformed nail is too extreme relative to your nail's shape, you may find it helpful to take the artificial nail, set it on a hard, flat surface, and press *lightly* downward on it, causing it to "spread", in effect making it less arched. Do this with care and do it gradually for best results.

There is a certain elasticity to these false nails that will allow them to be slightly flattened without fracturing. Do this until the false nail is reasonably similar to the curve of your true nail. It is advisable to avoid having a big "air pocket" between the real nail and the false nail as this gap makes the adhesive less effective, although not ineffective.

## Step 2: Attaching the Nails

Once the artificial nails are ready, you should then wash your real nails with rubbing alcohol to clean them completely as oils of any kind will weaken the adhesive's ability to bond. **This step is very important.** The adhesive "dot" is circular in shape and about the size of a dime. It comes on sheets of special paper that peel off easily. The dot is pressed firmly onto the surface of the fingernail where it will adhere.

The next step is to take the artificial nail and press it **hard** down onto the fingernail with the adhesive, making sure that it makes complete contact with the entire surface of the adhesive. As you press down on the false nail, move it very slightly from side to side to "cement" the bond between it, the adhesive and your real fingernail. If done correctly, the nail will be firmly attached and will not come off easily, even for hours. Of course, while wearing these nails you should avoid getting your hand wet.

## Step 3: Extra Protection—Clear Surgical Tape

But for a bit more insurance, a particular kind of tape called Nexcare Flexible Clear (also called Transpore Surgical Tape by 3M) can be used to cover the seam between the cuticle and the edge of the artificial nail. When playing a forceful, strong downward *rasgueado*, the back of the nail can "catch" on a string as you strum, causing the nail to go flying across the room! I experienced this and that is why I cover this seam. If you do not play much *rasgueado*, this step can be omitted as *punteado* playing does not present this potential problem.

## Step 4: Removing the Artificial Nail

The adhesive is strong enough to keep the false nail in place while playing, but will allow you to pry the false nail off relatively easily with no ill effects whatsoever to your fingernail when you are finished. The adhesive in most instances will stick to the false nail as it separates from the real nail. Whether it sticks to the false nail or your real nail, it is not difficult to peel it off completely from either surface. Follow the instructions given. Once this is done, the false nail will be "clean" and ready to use again. And there you are, back to normal instantly, with no bad side effects to your "living" nail.

# Advantages of Nonpermanent Adhesion of False Nails

The basic question is: how strong does the bond between the artificial nail and your real nail have to be in order to allow you to pluck and strum guitar strings effectively? The answer--not all that strong. The bonds produced by the chemicals in the synthetic systems described above all yield a very strong, practically indestructible type of adhesion (which is ironically part of the problem). In fact, I would call it "overkill". To play with a false nail, the bond only needs to be adequate for the need, which is the pressure exerted on the nail edge as it attacks and releases the string.

If you play guitar music that has extensive strumming, such as flamenco or Latin American repertoire, the RICONAIL system will definitely help. Strumming, or *rasgueado* technique, is particularly hard on the fingernails. That is because it is essentially a percussive "scraping" motion in both directions—very different from *punteado* (plucking technique), and a lot harder on the fingernails, I might add!

I primarily use fake nails to give my real nails a "rest" (as they are completely covered and protected in the RICONAIL system). I can thus avoid the "wear and tear" on my real nails that is an inevitable side effect of playing hours and hours every day. Now you have the freedom of choice, while avoiding all the problems of toxic adhesives.

Of course, if you have good natural nails, but happen to crack or damage a nail, the RICONAIL system will allow you to use a false nail temporarily and keep playing while your real nail grows out naturally with no hindrances. My artificial nail system will allow any guitarist (classical, jazz, acoustic fingerstyle, Latin Ameican or flamenco) to wear a false nail for any reason.

Just the other day I heard a scenario where my system might be the answer to a unique problem: a student at a music school is studying both organ and guitar. Having longer nails on her right hand inhibits her keyboard playing. She needs to be able to put on false nails temporarily for her guitar practice, and then take them off to play the organ. Voila! Her problem is solved with the RICONAIL system.

# Ode to Nontoxicity

I do not relate to cyanoacrilate.
But I have a date to play at eight
So I cannot wait.

My nails should be in an optimum state
If I really want to sound first rate.
So how am I to avoid cyanoacrilate?

RICONAILS will demonstrate
How to escape cyanoacrilate
With a safe, new method that works just great!

# Chapter 5: Shaping and Polishing the Nails

It has been said that **nails are the guitarist's bow**. Nails that are strong, flexible and tough, of the right length and always in a highly polished state are like a good bow to a violin virtuoso. Getting your nails in optimum shape is relatively inexpensive; thank goodness you do not have to spend thousands of dollars to have a good "bow"!

For many years I used a "Diamond Dust" or "Sapphire Dust" nail file to shape my nails. These files are available at any drug store. As files go, they are less destructive on your nails compared to traditional nail files or emery boards, which should be avoided at all costs. I also used Tri-m-ite 500 grit open coat silicon carbide sandpaper from 3M to polish my nails.

Now I employ a different system that is superior to the methods cited above. In fact, I use a diamond dust file only when absolutely necessary, avoiding it 95% of the time. What I use now is polishing cloth coated with tiny abrasive crystals on resilient cloth-backed latex. These "cushioned" particles generate less heat and friction, and last much longer than regular sandpaper. Credit for this discovery goes to John Sutherland of Georgia who put together "Sutherland's Nail Kit". It consists of three 4 x 2.5 inch swaths of polishing cloth in three grits: 2500, 4000 and 12000. Also included is a special rectangular piece of foam-like material (approximately 1 x 1 x 3 inches) that is just right in terms of not being too soft or too hard.

The polishing cloth swatches wrap around the rectangular foam block, allowing a good surface for shaping and polishing your nails. Both the foam block surface and the rubber undercoating on the polishing cloth "give" when pressure is applied, and this allows you to sand and shape with much less stress on the nail tip, taking off very small amounts of nail material in all three phases, achieving a polished surface that is practically "mirror-like" in its smoothness and certainly superior to what you can get with 500 grit open coat silicon carbide. The 2500 grit polishing cloth is used to shape, the 4000 grit is used to smooth out any roughness, and the 12000 is for a high gloss finish. And believe me, it works!

I have also used a very fine wet stone (for sharpening knives) to polish the free edge of my nails. This works quite well, but the stone surface is in fact very dense and has no give to it whatsoever.

Nail length is a matter of preference. I find that when my nails are about as long or just a wee bit longer than the end of the fingertip, they work the best. Nails that are too long can be problematic. It has been stated that your nails should extend 1/16th inch beyond the end of the fingertip with the thumbnail up to 1/8th of an inch longer. I like a long thumbnail, but it is probably the most difficult nail to grow out fairly long due to the fact that the physics of the thumb stroking forcefully downward create a different kind of motion and stress compared to the "upward" stroke utilized by the other fingers.

I shape my nails a certain way to achieve the desired tone quality- bright and "fat" with good projection. For right-handed players, there are four basic ways of shaping the nail: A. Stroke from the left side with a non-symmetrical curve, lower at left side; B. Stroke from the left with a straight left–to-right ramp shape; C. Stroke from the right side with a rounded nail, lower at right; D. Stroke from the right with a ramp shape. I play from the left side of my fingertips using shape A, flattening a small area at the exact spot where the string is released to facilitate that release. Every guitarist must develop his or her own formula for nail length and shape according to subjective and personal criteria, taking into account tone quality and right-hand technique. Above all, experiment and listen!

A         B         C         D

# A Short History of Fingernail Care

**1800-** Almond-shaped nails, short and slightly pointed, are the fashion ideal. Nails are sometimes tinted with scented red oil and buffed with a chamois cloth.

**1830-** In Europe, a foot doctor named Sitts develops the orangewood stick, adapted from a dental tool, for nails. Before this invention, metal tools, acid and scissors were used to manicure nails.

**1892-** Dr. Sitts' niece brings nail care to women, and the Sitts method reaches the U.S. salons catering to women of different incomes.

**1900-** Women clip their nails with metal scissors and file their nails with metal files. Tinted creams or powders are massaged into the nails to create shine. A glossy nail varnish is made available and is applied with a camel hair brush. It wears off in a day.

**1910-** Flowery Manicure Products is established around 1910 in New York City. The company manufactures metal nail files and invents and introduces the emery board (garnet abrasive on a wood center).

**1914-** Anne Kindred of North Dakota files a patent for a fingernail shield, a covering for the nails designed to protect them from discoloring while the wearer works with chemicals or other discoloring agents.

**1920-** Screen stars are known for a total look that is almost childlike, with short hair and slender figures. Nails are still unpolished, but soon the development of automobile paint provides the basis for fingernail paint.

**1925-** Nail Polish enters the market in a sheer rosy red shade and is applied only to the center of the nail. The moon and the free edge are left colorless.

**1927-** Max Factor introduces Society Nail Tint, a small porcelain pot containing rose colored cream. Applied to the nail and buffed, it gives a natural rose color.

**1932-** Charles Revson, with his brother and chemist Joseph Revson, and Charles Lachman, creates an opaque, non-streaking nail polished based on pigments rather than dyes, making a variety of colors available. Revlon is born.

**1934-** Max Factor's "Liquid Nail Enamel" is introduced and is similar to nail polishes of today.

**1937-** A patent for a method using tips to repair and lengthen the nails is granted to Harriet Fligenbaum

**1940-** Rita Hayworth's long red nails bring new shape to nail fashions.

**1945-** Max Factor offers "Satin Smooth Nail Polish" to consumers. An improvement upon it's earlier Liquid Nail Enamel, the polish is available in reds, pinks and other colors.

**1950-** Juliette Marglen markets a wrap material resembling a match-book with the wrap material in sheets. Only the top third of the nail is covered.

**957-** Thomas Slack is issued a patent for a "platform" that fits around the nail edge, designed to help manicurists apply extensions to the natural nail. Made of foil, it is used to apply the first acrylic for nails, called "Patinail", which is manufactured in the fifties by the Slack family.

**959-** Max Factor's "Nail Enamel" is introduced.

**960-** False nails make their entrance, and they are longer than ever. Silk and linen wraps are found to be stronger than paper wraps. Mona Nail, a Dallas company, manufactures one of the earliest acrylic systems for nails.

**970-** The age of the artificial nail. Acrylic nails look and feel real, but are much stronger. The square nail evolves. Artificial nails that cover the entire nail bed are available including the Eye-Lure Nails brand. These are inserted under a lifted cuticle to make them look as if they grow out of the finger. Glue holds them on but not for long as water dissolves the glue.

**971-** GG's Nails System is founded and starts with linen and fiberglass wraps.

**973-** IBD develops the first adhesive especially for fingernails.

**974 & 1975-** The FDA seizes and recalls products containing methyl methacrylate, a chemical considered to be hazardous, and forces manufactures to reformulate acrylics.

**980-** The eighties sees the use of nail drills (adapted from dental, hobby and jewelry drills) that become common when working with acrylic nails. Fiberglass is the newest wrap system- light, strong & flexible.

**983-** Heken Gourley offers one of the new gel systems on the market.

**985-** Lee Pharmaceuticals introduces Lee Press-On Nails, which are applied with adhesive tabs.

**2005-** Rico Stover offers a new way to attach a false nail that is nontoxic, nonpermanent and strong enough for guitar players to wear for hours.

# List of Manufacturers

**American International Industries**
2220 Gaspar Avenue
Commerce, CA 90040
323 728-2999
www.aiibeauty.com

**Aquarian Treasures**
5605 Shore Blvd., Gulfport Beach, FL 33707
727 347-0623 winter or 814 474-5356 summer
www.smartnails.com
SmartNail@aol.com

**Black Pearl Botanicals**
22 Calle de Maya
Placitas, NM 87043
505 867-9606
www.blackpearlbotanicals.com
jillg@blackpearlbotanicals.com

**Botanical Skin Works**
1709 Fleet St., 2nd floor, suite 2
Baltimore, MD 21231-2917
410 675 2006
www.botanicalworks.com
info@botanicalworks.com

**Dairy Association Company Incorporated**
91 Williams St
Lyndonville, VT 05851
802 626-3610
www.bagbalm.com
info@bagbalm.com

**Dartmouth Pharmaceuticals, Inc.**
38 Church Ave.
Wareham, MA 02751
800 414 3566/508 295 2200
www.ilovemynails.com
info@ilovemynails.com

**De Lore Nails**
(see **American International Corporation**)
www.aiibeauty.com/delore.html

**Earth Therapuetics , Ltd.**
POB 1009 Plainview, NY 11803
www.earththerapuetics.com

**Fingernailcare.com**
578 Hilton Memory Road
Vidalia, GA 30474
912 538 7028
www.fingernailcare.com
barbara@fingernailcare.com

**Gena Laboratories**
(see **American International Corporation**)
www.aiibeauty.com/gena.html

**Herbal Luxuries Natural Skin Care**
POB 820 Pelham, AL 35124-0820
866 825 6584
www.herballuxuries.com

**HMS Crown, Inc.**
550 Vista Drive
Ridgway, CO 81432
800 867 7897
www.hmscrown.com
anti-aging@hmscrown.com

**ibd** (see **American International Corporation**)
www.ibdbeauty.com

**Isabella**
2780 Via Orange Way, Suite B
Spring Valley, CA 91978 USA
800 777 5205
www.isabella-catalog.net
service@isabellacatalog.net

**Nailtiques**
12415 SW 136th Ave.
Miami, FL 33186
800 272 0054/305 378-0740
www.nailtiques.com
mail@nailtiques.com

Nature's Plus (Natural Organics)
48 Broadhollow Rd.
Melville, NY 11747-3708
31 293 0030
www.naturesplus.com

Nature's Plus
48 Broadhollow Road
Melville, NY 11747
www.naturesplus.com

Onyx Laboratories
N. Little Rock, AK 72113
01 753 7676

ProStrong Inc.
0 Main Street
Oakville, CT 06779
77 678 7664
www.prostrong.com
atorderdesk@prostrong.com

Rainbow Research Corporation
70 Wilbur Place
Bohemia, NY 11716
800 722 9595/631 589 5563
www.rainbowresearch.com
info@rainbowresearch.com

Sally Beauty Worldwide Headquarters
3001 Colorado Blvd.
Denton, Texas 76210
940 898 7643
www.sallybeauty.com

Skin Biology Incorporated
12833 S.E. 40th Place
Bellevue, WA 98006
800 405 1912
www.bioheal.com
help@bioheal.com

Source Océan Institute
8 Vista Drive, Old Lyme, CT 06371
800 365 3958
www.wilkesgroup.com
mail@wilkesgroup.com

The Tetra Corporation
POB 940 Dumfries, VA 22026
800 826 0479
www.TheTetraCorporation.com
info@thetetracorporation.com
www.onymyrrhe.com

Trind Nail & Hand Corporation
1715 Lakeside Avenue #8
St Augustine, FL 32084
866 874 6326
www.trendnailandhand.com
trindrh@earthlink.net

Wildlands Beauty Products
POB 683 Santa Fe, NM 87504
505 988 4509

W. S. Badger Company Inc.
P.O. Box 58 Gilsum, NH 03448
800 603 6100/603 357 2958
www.badgerbalm.com
info@badgerbalm.com

Internet Sources for Pure Oils:

Monterey Bay Spice Company
www.herbco.com
800 500 6148

Mountain Rose Herbs
www.mountainroseherbs.com
800 879 3337

Nail Polishing:

John Sutherland
Nail Filing/Polishing System
4179 Luis Ct. Snellville, GA 30039
770 972 5775
johnsuth@mindspring.com

Custom False Nails:

True Fit Nails
2550 S 2300 W Suite #1
West Valley City, UT 84119
801 924 0002
www.truefitnails.com

**Artificial Nails with Nontoxic Adhesive:**

*FROM RICONAILS*
## *Emergency Nail Kit*

*Available from Mel Bay Accessories:*
**www.melbay.com**

*Also available from:*

RICONAILS
www.ricoguitarnails.com
or
www.quericopub.com

Disclaimer: The manufacturers listed above were all operating and in business at the time that this book was created. However, due to the incessant vicissitudes of the free market, no guarantee is given that these businesses will continue to offer the products cited here at the time the reader consults the information given.

# Bibliography

**Books:**

Dadd, Debra Lynn, *Home Safe Home*, Tarcher/Putnam, New York (1977).

Erickson, Kim, *Drop Dead Gorgeous*, Contemporary Books, McGraw Hill (2002).

Hampton, Aubrey, *Natural Organic Hair and Skin Care*, Organica Press, Tampa (1987).

Vance, Judi, *Beauty to Die For: The Cosmetic Consequence*, iUniverse, Lincoln, NE (2000).

Winter, Ruth, *The Consumer's Dictionary of Cosmetic Ingredients*, Three Rivers, New York (1999)

**Articles:**

Counter Intelligence," Erickson, Kim, Delicious Living, March 2003, p. 80.

Cosmetic Safety: More Complex Than at First Blush", FDA Consumer, November 1991.

**Internet sources:**

www.detox.org/e-fattyacids.html

www.judithbennhurley.com/rxforridnail.html

www.rxwellnesscenter.com/Hair_Skin_Nails.asp

www.heall.com/skinhair.html

www.madsci.org/posts/archives/jun99/929465183.An.r.html

www.nail-solutions.co.uk/Nail%20anatomy.htm

http://jeb.biologists.org/cgi/content/full/207/5/735

http://members.aol.com/alligal/nail1on/mma.htm

www.fpnotebook.com/DER65.htm

http://home.iprimus.com.au/gjdemontfort/Aromatherapy.htm

www.naildr.com/History.html

www.beautytech.info/articles/latimes1-28-00.htm

www.beautytech.com/articles/mmafactsheet.html

www.altru.org/healthyliving/familyhome/nov03familyhomefingernails.htmcc

# Other Publications by Rico Stover

**Latin American Guitar Guide (95478BCD)**

This is a well written, informative study of the solo and rhythmic guitar styles found in Latin America. Featured is music from Argentina, Brazil, Costa Rica, Paraguay, Peru, and Venezuela. Most of the compositions are in E major or E minor and all are scored in notation and tablature.

**Barrios in Tablature Volume 1 (95705BCD)**

Augustin Barrios was one of the greatest geniuses who ever played and composed music for the guitar. This book features a variety of his works ranging from the moderately easy to complex. In addition to being excellent technique studies, these compositions are wonderful solo pieces that reflect the impressionistic, Latin, and European influences found in the unique Barrios compositional style.

**The Complete Works of Barrios Volume 1 (96308)**

The product of decades of scholarly investigation, Volume 1 contains 67 musical works by the virtuoso Paraguayan guitarist Agustín Barrios Mangoré (1885-1944). This is the first edition of Barrios' music based on all available sources: manuscripts, phonograph recordings and published editions (pre-1970s). Written in standard notation only, the two volumes of this definitive collection are illustrated with period photographs, concert programs and Barrios' own drawings. The legacy of Barrios is one of the most important and outstanding contributions ever made to the classic guitar, and it is with great pride that Mel Bay Publications offers here for the first time in one edition the collected works of Agustín Barrios Mangoré.

**The Complete Works of Barrios Volume 2 (20765BCD)**

Volume 2 of this landmark publication includes 65 original compositions in standard notation plus a unique CD featuring Barrios himself playing 21 original works including: Danza Paraguaya, La Catedral, Un Sueño en la Floresta, Maxixe, Tarantella, Aire Popular Paraguayo and many more! In addition to the music, 82 pages of exhaustive Critical Notes shed light on the Barrios catalog making this the definitive anthology of his work. More reliable, comprehensive and articulate than any previously published edition, this new Mel Bay Publications compilation (524 pages in all) will make the entire world of Barrios more accessible.